HEAVEN'S HILL
MEETING YOUR LOVED ONES ON THE OTHER SIDE

G.W EVANS

HEAVEN'S HILL

Meeting your Loved Ones on the Other Side

by

G.W. Evans

Copyright Notice

For those I've loved and lost, both two and four legged, I miss and love you deeply, and more than words can express. I am right behind you. See you on the other side.

TABLE OF CONTENTS

ONE

Meeting Beyond the Horizon

This book is about what we hope is waiting for all of us on 'the other side'. It is not a religious book; nor is it devoted to any form of Absolute Being or deity.

I believe there is light right from the start of leaving this earthly space with Heaven's Hill just a short distance away.

What is Heaven's Hill?

Close your eyes for a few minutes and try to relax. Envisage the people you have loved in your life; young, old, acquaintances, relatives, friends, lovers, and don't forget the awesome, furry members of the family who have passed on. The common denominator or link is you.

You knew them all in some way and they all knew you. You had relationships with them; some of which were loving, enriching, and deeply satisfying, and others that may have been toxic to your system, soul destroying or even dangerous. Nevertheless, there was a relationship of some kind that affected you as well as them.

They are gone now – have they changed since you knew them? Are they still the same people you spent time with on earth? Do you really want to know?

Now, try to imagine all these souls at the best times of their healthy lives spread out on a high grassy knoll on a stunningly, beautiful, sunny day, talking, laughing, and getting to know one another. They are joyful, happy, and open to the other souls sitting on the knoll. They are talking about you and are there for one purpose – to await your arrival and welcome you with excitement and the love you have missed so much. They have changed from the last time you saw them, and so have you.

You can see them as if they were alive at the height of good health and happiness; feel their love, and allow it to bring you closer to them, and them to you. Can you see your pets? They are mingling with everyone on the Hill, playing, running around or laying on the grass catching the sun's rays. As we grow older, we move closer to being with them all again in a wonderous, magical place that I call Heaven's Hill.

It could be morning, or evening, afternoon or anytime at all. It has nothing to do with your age, but with your memories and feelings for all those who have gone before you. Close friends and family, pets, and others we have seen pass through time and space to another dimension. I have seen many – more than my fair share over the years; some in clusters during a short span of time, individuals when it was simply their time to move on and more taken too early from their busy lives. Have you experienced this progression?

We can see them and hear their voices, each one, their smiles and laughs, shapes of their bodies and faces, and their hair colors, clothes, and styles. There is no language barrier, no matter where they originated, because there is a deeper understanding, and communication is easy and fluid.

I first saw them all in a dream a long time ago, but I have dreamed regularly about them since in my sleep and in daydreams. All of them, including my beloved pets, sitting on a bright green grassy hill on a sunny day with large white, puffy clouds overhead. The temperature is warm, not hot, not cool, just perfect. They were each sitting with crossed legs or laying straight out on the soft turf, walking around, or bending over talking to other souls, introducing themselves by saying "I'm so and so, who are you?". They did not have to mention me – everyone there was aware of my connection; it was understood, a given. There is an enormous feeling of elation and anticipation, which is almost tangible, as I continue to dream about Heaven's Hill.

I was incredibly fortunate to have people of all ages, ethnic groups, races, and religions in my life. They taught me so much and gave generously of themselves. Many are gone now – gone to Heaven's Hill where they sit around talking and laughing and looking toward the distance knowing that I am very close to joining them.

There are too many to discuss individually, but each one remains fresh in my mind and loved with all my heart. The ones that shocked my system to its core with hurt and pain at sometimes during my life are also there, but they appear to have changed. They have rid themselves of whatever it was that caused them to hurt and to induce pain in me and others. They have found their reason for being. I simply feel at peace for them and myself.

TWO

Finding Purpose and Shedding the Past

As we journey through life, we often wonder about the purpose of our existence. We question the trials and tribulations we face, the joys and sorrows we experience. But on Heaven's Hill, these questions find their answers. The souls there have found their purpose, their reason for being. They have shed the layers of hurt, pain, and misunderstanding that once clouded their existence. They have embraced love, forgiveness, and understanding.

Imagine them, these souls you once knew, free from the burdens of their past. They are no longer defined by their mistakes, their failures, or their regrets. Instead, they are defined by their love for you, their anticipation of your arrival. They are defined by the joy they feel knowing they will soon be reunited with you.

They are there, waiting for you, not impatiently, but with a serene sense of knowing. Time, as we understand it, does not exist on Heaven's Hill. There is no rush, no urgency. There is only the gentle flow of existence, the peaceful passage of moments filled with love and anticipation.

The Reunion on the Hill

Picture this scenario:

During a severe illness, I found myself slipping into unconsciousness. Suddenly, I was standing on a lush, green hill under a bright, sunny sky. The air was warm and fragrant with the scent of blooming flowers. In the distance, I saw a group of people gathered, their faces filled with joy and anticipation.

As I walked closer, I recognized them—my parents, who had passed away when I was young, and my childhood dog, Max, who bounded towards me with excitement. My parents embraced me, and I felt a wave of love and comfort wash over me. Max wagged his tail and nuzzled my hand, just as he used to.

We sat together on the Hill, reminiscing about old times and sharing stories. My parents looked younger and healthier than I remembered, their faces glowing with happiness. They told me about the wonderful place they now called home and assured me that we would be together again someday.

As the sun began to set, they gently told me it was time to go back. I felt a tug, and the hill began to fade. I woke up in my hospital bed, tears of joy streaming down my face. The experience left me with a deep sense of peace and the knowledge that our loved ones are always with us, waiting to welcome us home.

As you move closer to the time when you will join others in your life who have passed, you might feel a sense of apprehension. But let that apprehension be tempered by the knowledge that you are not moving towards an unknown. You are moving towards a reunion with those you have loved and lost. You are moving towards a place of love, understanding, and acceptance.

Can you remember a time when you felt the presence of a departed friend, loved one or pet? The sense that they were there, in the same space as you? Were you able to feel them or smell their familiar scent? This is a common experience of those sensitive to the departed.

The Whisper of the Past

Can you see yourself in the following scene?

As the sun dipped below the horizon, casting a warm glow through the old oak trees, Linda sat on the porch of her family home. The evening air was cool, and the gentle breeze rustled the leaves, creating a soothing symphony. It had been almost a year since her father had passed away, yet the memory of him remained vivid in her heart.

This evening felt different, though. After Linda finished her mug of Chamomile tea, she went to bed. She was sleeping well until 2 AM when she felt an inexplicable presence in standing beside her. The room was dark, but she wasn't afraid. She simply had a feeling -an almost tangible awareness, that her father was standing right next to her watching her sleep.

Linda's eyes remained closed, but the familiar scent of her dad's cologne wafted through the air, mixing with the stuffiness in the bedroom. She opened her eyes, and a shadow of a form passed quickly and disappeared. Somehow, she wasn't surprised.

A sense of peace washed over her. Linda knew he was there with her, in spirit; She smiled and sat up with her legs over the side of the bed. Suddenly, she felt a soft brush against her legs. Looking down, she saw nothing, but she knew it was Remy, her beloved Collie, who had passed away a few years earlier. Remy had always slept by her side during the night, and her presence now was as real as ever. She could almost feel her fur against her skin and see her brown, soulful eyes looking up at her.

Tears welled up in Linda's eyes, but they were tears of joy and gratitude. In this magical moment, she felt connected to her father and Remy. The lines between the physical and spiritual world blurred, and Linda knew that love transcended even death. This experience reassured her that those we love never truly leave us; their presence remains a part of us, always and forever.

As sleep descended upon her again, Linda whispered a heartfelt thank you to her father and Remy. She felt their love surround her, giving her strength and comfort. And with that, she knew she was never alone and would be with them again when her time was ready.

As you continue your journey through life, carry this image with you. The image of your loved ones on Heaven's Hill, bathed in the warm glow of a perfect day, their faces lit up with joy and anticipation. Let this image fill you with peace and hope. Let it remind you that at the end of your earthly journey, a new journey awaits. A journey that begins on Heaven's Hill.

Remember, the souls on Heaven's Hill have changed, and so have you. You have grown, learned, and evolved. And when the time comes for you to join them, you, too, will shed your burdens, and you'll experience the joy and love that awaits on Heaven's Hill.

The Essence of a Universal Language

Telepathy and Empathy: In the realm of souls, communication might occur through telepathy—a direct transfer of thoughts, emotions, and intentions from one soul to another. This method eliminates the need for spoken language, allowing for a purer, more immediate connection. Empathy plays a significant role here, as souls are able to fully understand and share each other's feelings without the distortion that sometimes comes with words.

Energy and Vibration: Every soul emits a unique energy or vibration, which can be sensed and interpreted by other souls. This energy carries the essence of one's being, including emotions, intentions, and even memories. By tuning into these vibrations, souls can communicate their deepest thoughts and feelings effortlessly.

Some of us are fortunate enough to have a heightened sensitivity to this universal language, which makes it easier feel the presence of some of those souls who have passed. Have you ever experienced a sense of foreboding and then received a phone call or message that someone close to you had passed away? It's not uncommon.

Connecting Beyond Words

Shared Experiences: Souls in the afterlife may share experiences in a way that transcends individual perspectives. This shared understanding creates a deep sense of connection and community. For example, a soul might relive a cherished memory with another, allowing both to experience the joy and emotion of that moment simultaneously.

Collective Consciousness: The idea of a collective consciousness suggests that all souls are part of a greater, interconnected whole. In this state, individual identities blend with the collective, enabling souls to access and contribute to a vast repository of knowledge and experience. Communication within this collective consciousness is seamless and instantaneous, as all souls are attuned to the same frequency of understanding.

Pure Emotional Exchange: Beyond words, communication in the afterlife could involve the direct exchange of emotions. Souls might share feelings of love, joy, or peace through a direct emotional connection, creating an intense and immediate bond. This form of communication allows for a depth of understanding that surpasses verbal expression.

Practical Implications

Healing and Reconciliation: A universal language allows for healing and reconciliation in the afterlife. Souls can communicate their true feelings and intentions without the limitations of spoken language, resolving past conflicts and finding peace. This deep understanding fosters forgiveness and acceptance, contributing to the overall harmony of the afterlife.

Personal Growth: Communicating beyond words facilitates personal growth and spiritual development. Souls can share insights and experiences that lead to greater self-awareness and understanding. This exchange of wisdom helps each soul evolve and progress on their spiritual journey.

Unconditional Love: At the core of a universal language is the expression of unconditional love. Souls are able to convey and receive love in its purest form, unencumbered by misunderstandings or misinterpretations. This love strengthens the bonds between souls, creating a sense of unity and belonging.

The idea of a universal language in the afterlife suggests a form of communication that transcends the limitations of words, allowing souls to connect on a deep, intuitive level. Through telepathy, shared experiences, and direct emotional exchange, souls are able to understand and support each other in ways that are both profound and comforting.

This concept not only offers a glimpse into the nature of the afterlife but also highlights the enduring power of love and connection that transcends all boundaries. This is Heaven's Hill.

THREE

What is Heaven's Hill?

What do we know about Heaven's Hill? Where did the image come from, how long has it been there, and could it be real? It is real if you believe it is real, and then it becomes real. It's a place where you can be happy and fulfilled by being with the ones who have meant so much but passed before you.

Heaven's Hill is a deeply personal and spiritual concept. It's a place of comfort and peace, a sanctuary for the souls of those we've loved and lost. The image of Heaven's Hill comes from our hearts and minds, shaped by our memories, beliefs, and hopes.

The concept of Heaven's Hill has been there as long as we've sought to understand and find comfort in the cycle of life and death. It becomes real through our belief and imagination. It's a place where we can feel connected to those who have passed on, imagining them at their best, free from earthly struggles.

Heaven's Hill is for everyone who has lost someone, pets, or more than just one soul in their lives. It's a place as wide as the universe with space for each of us. My 'compartment' on the Hill is green, wide, on a soft earth with the warmth from the sun. Heaven's Hill extends as far as those who knew me and as wide.

My vision of Heaven's Hill, a wide, green space bathed in warm sunlight, reflects my personal vision of peace and happiness. Others might envision their own compartments differently, perhaps as a serene beach or a mountaintop with crisp, clear air.

Where is your compartment in Heaven's Hill? Do you see your people waiting on a white, sandy beach facing a calm, blue green ocean, or are they waiting at the top of a flat top mountain where the air is crisp and clear?

What are the shapes of those on Heaven's Hill? Are they bodies and faces, or are they floating souls with vibrating auras? They are as you imagine them. I imagine them as if they were at their best, but you might see them as auras, connecting through colors or vibes. It makes no difference; they are your souls to visualize as you wish in the form to which you can best relate.

The souls on Heaven's Hill can take any form that brings us comfort and feels most real to us. They could be envisioned as human forms, vibrant auras, or even ethereal shapes. The key is that these forms resonate with our personal experiences and relationships with those souls.

In essence, Heaven's Hill is a testament to the enduring power of love and memory. It's a place where every soul is welcome, where every soul can find peace. It's not just for the chosen few, but for everyone who has loved and been loved. It's a place shaped by our beliefs, our memories, and our hopes for what lies beyond the realm of the living. Heaven's Hill is indeed your vision, a vision of love, peace, and reunion.

FOUR

Our 4-Legged Family of Souls

Our Pet Family

The relationship between people and their beloved pets is extraordinary; it encompasses feelings of devotion and such deep love that they are almost tangible – you can feel this love from the depth of your soul while it stands right in front of you. No matter whether it's a dog or cat, bird, fish, horse, turtle or another creature – love is love.

Pets have an extraordinary ability to provide unconditional love and comfort, which can greatly enhance our well-being and quality of life. They offer companionship, affection, and loyalty without expecting anything in return. This bond between humans and animals is profound and deeply rooted in our shared history.

Can you imagine the following?

When I opened my eyes, I felt a warm breeze on my face and soft grass under my feet. I looked around the Hill on which I found myself and saw a beautiful garden full of flowers and trees. I heard a familiar bark and turned to see my old dog, Jax, a shiny, blond Labrador Retriever, running towards me. He jumped on me with his strong, 60lb body, licking my face, furiously fanning his tail. I hugged him and cried like a baby. I had missed him so much. He looked healthy, and so happy to see me!

Jax turned, so I followed his gaze and saw more of my old pets coming out of the bushes and trees, running down the grass verges and hills coming to meet me! I recognized them all. They were all the pets I had loved and lost over the years. There were Squishy and Parts, my first cats, who died of old age, and my favorites, Yancy, Mia and Ace, bounding through the green grass.

14

15

I could see Chewy, my rabbit, who got sick before she finally closed her eyes, and Squawk, my parrot, who flew away and never came back. I even saw Yam, my Goldfish, who got flushed down the toilet when it died. Yam was in a small tank on wheels, rolling down a short hill toward me. There were more, too many to name. They all came to me and greeted me with such joy and affection. I felt overwhelmed by their love and happiness, and we all cried together.

I couldn't stop smiling and felt a peace and joy that I had never felt before. I knew I was home. I knew I was in heaven. I knew I was with my all my loved ones and pet family. I was happy. I was on Heaven's Hill.

Scientific Insights into the Human-Animal Bond

1. Oxytocin Release

The strong human-animal bond triggers the release of Oxytocin, often referred to as the "love hormone." because it's responsible for some positive emotions, such as attraction and sexual desire. It's also responsible for things such as contractions during labor, breast milk release when feeding, trust, and happiness. Oxytocin plays a key role in social bonding, stress relief, and emotional well-being, so petting a dog or cat can increase the levels in both the pet and the owner, creating a mutual sense of calm and happiness.

2. Stress Reduction

Because interactions with pets can significantly reduce stress and anxiety, spending time with animals lowers cortisol levels, the hormone associated with stress. This effect is so strong that therapy animals are often used in hospitals, nursing homes, and schools provide emotional support and reduce anxiety.

3. Emotional Support

Pets provide a sense of purpose and routine, which can be particularly beneficial for individuals dealing with depression or loneliness. The simple act of caring for a pet - feeding them, taking them for walks, or playing with them can give individuals a sense of responsibility and a reason to get out of bed in the morning.

4. Social Interaction

Pets can also facilitate social interactions. Taking a dog for a walk, for example, often leads to conversations with other dog owners and passersby. This can help build a sense of community and reduce feelings of isolation.

5. Physical Health Benefits

Beyond emotional support, pets contribute to physical health as well. Dog owners, in particular, tend to get more exercise due to regular walks. This can lead to lower blood pressure, loss of weight, and a stronger immune system.

The Special Bond with Dogs and Cats

Dogs

Dogs have been bred over thousands of years to be loyal companions to humans. Their ability to read human emotions and respond with empathy makes them especially effective in providing comfort and support. Service dogs, for instance, can be trained to assist people with disabilities, while therapy dogs provide emotional support to those in need.

Cats

Cats, while often more independent than dogs, form deep bonds with their owners as well. They appear to be aloof, but they actually get very attached to their owners. They are known for their soothing purrs, which can have a calming effect on humans, and can even promote healing and reduce pain.

Conclusion

The bond between humans and all types of pets is both unique and powerful. Pets offer unconditional and unwavering love, providing immense comfort and joy. The scientific community has increasingly recognized the profound impact that animals have on our emotional and physical well-being, further highlighting the importance of these cherished companions in our lives.

The Soul in Animals

Is there an afterlife Rainbow Bridge for Pets?[2]

Whether you call it a Rainbow Bridge or another name, many believe that our pets cross and enter it, and from there, eventually, we reunite with them on Heaven's Hill. For those lost, abused or homeless animals, people on Heaven's Hill welcome them with open, loving arms, where they are cherished and spoiled like all the others.

1. **Shared Essence:** Some spiritual perspectives argue that animals possess souls similar to humans. They believe that our souls come from the same oversouls. In this view, your oversoul isn't confined to your body alone; it also inhabits other human bodies and even animals.

2. **Distinct Differences:** Animal souls are distinct from human souls. Animals don't directly reflect the likeness of humans; although their souls serve a different purpose, they continue to exist forever, just like human souls.

3. **Ensouled Matter:** Animals exhibit characteristics of ensouled matter. This means that their behavior, emotions, and interconnectedness with nature suggest a deeper essence beyond mere biological processes. Often deeper than humans.

Whether you believe in the soul as a spiritual essence or view it through a scientific lens, the concept remains a profound mystery. Perhaps wisdom lies in embracing both perspectives—the poetic and the empirical—as we explore the enigma of existence[13,14,15,16].

Always there for us, pets are ready to provide comfort and joy. Whether it's a dog greeting you excitedly at the door, a cat curling up on your lap, or a bird singing sweetly in the morning, the love pets give is pure. Reuniting with them again on Heaven's Hill is heaven itself.

FIVE

The Mystery of Passing Over

The mystery of what lies beyond death is something that has intrigued humanity for centuries. While we may not have definitive answers, the hope and comfort that many find in the idea of being reunited with loved ones and cherished pets in a place of peace and love, like Heaven's Hill, is truly powerful. It's a testament to the enduring bonds of love and companionship that we form during our lives. These bonds, it seems, are so strong that they transcend the physical realm and continue to live on in our hearts and minds.

You can realize that idea simply by focusing on your vision of Heaven's Hill. The power of visualization is profound. By focusing on your personal vision of Heaven's Hill, you can create a sense of peace and comfort within yourself. This mental image can serve as a source of solace during challenging times, reminding you of the enduring bonds of love and companionship that transcend our physical existence. It's a beautiful way to keep the memory of your loved ones alive and close to your heart while imagining a joyous reunion with all of them on your arrival.

There is no longer any need to be afraid of leaving this life. The concept of Heaven's Hill, so real to me that I feel I know every blade of grass, each white puffy cloud floating in the blue, blue sky, provides a hugely comforting perspective on the transition from our earthly existence to what lies beyond. It's a place of love, peace, and reunion, free from fear and uncertainty. The belief in Heaven's Hill brings solace, and eliminates the fear associated with the unknown. Remember, our loved ones are there, waiting for us, ready to welcome us with open arms.

What is it like when you pass?

Although no one knows for certain, we can learn from envisioning Heaven's Hill.

1. **Embracing the Continuity of Love:** Envisioning Heaven's Hill highlights the enduring nature of love. It teaches us that love transcends physical boundaries and persists beyond life. Recognizing this can encourage us to cherish and nurture our relationships, knowing that the bonds we form are eternal.

2. **Finding Comfort and Peace:** The concept of Heaven's Hill provides a comforting and peaceful view of the afterlife. It alleviates fears and anxieties about death by presenting a beautiful, welcoming place where we are reunited with loved ones. This perspective can bring solace to those grieving or facing the end of life.

3. **Healing and Reconciliation:** Imagining a place where souls meet in harmony and joy encourages us to seek healing and reconciliation in our current relationships. It prompts us to mend rifts, forgive past grievances, and build meaningful connections, knowing that these efforts contribute to our inner peace and the peace of those we love.

4. **Embracing Diversity:** Heaven's Hill is envisioned as a place where people of all ages, backgrounds, and experiences come together. This inclusivity teaches us to value and respect diversity in our lives, fostering a sense of unity and acceptance.

5. **Living with Purpose:** Understanding that our actions and relationships carry forward into the afterlife can inspire us to live with greater purpose and intention. It encourages us to make choices that align with our values and to engage in acts of kindness and compassion.

Impact on Our Lives Now

1. **Enhancing Relationships:** Believing in a reunion with loved ones encourages us to prioritize our relationships. We become more present, attentive, and loving towards those around us, knowing that these connections are precious and everlasting.

2. **Cultivating Inner Peace:** The vision of Heaven's Hill as a place of peace and joy can inspire us to cultivate these qualities in our daily lives. We learn to let go of unnecessary worries and focus on what truly matters, fostering a sense of inner calm and contentment.

3. **Encouraging Kindness and Empathy:** Knowing that we are part of a larger, interconnected whole encourages us to act with kindness and empathy. We become more aware of the impact of our actions on others and strive to create positive ripples in the world.

4. **Finding Hope and Optimism:** Envisioning a beautiful afterlife can fill us with hope and optimism. It reminds us that there is more to life than our immediate struggles and that a brighter, happier existence awaits us. This hope can sustain us through difficult times and inspire us to persevere.

5. **Motivating Personal Growth:** The idea of spiritual growth and development in the afterlife motivates us to pursue personal growth now. We seek to better ourselves, develop our character, and deepen our understanding of life and love.

Envisioning Heaven's Hill as a place of peace, love, and reunion provides a positive reflection of what lies ahead. It not only offers comfort and hope but also encourages us to live our lives with greater purpose, kindness, and connection. By internalizing these lessons, we can create a more fulfilling and meaningful existence, both for ourselves and for those we cherish.

SIX

Heaven Among Cultures

Although my view of Heaven's Hill may well be different than others, different cultures and traditions have various ways of imagining the afterlife and what it means to reunite with loved ones who have passed away. The following are just some of the examples of how different cultures and traditions imagine the afterlife and what it means to reunite with loved ones who have passed away:

In **Hinduism**, the afterlife is determined by one's karma and actions in life. The soul undergoes a cycle of rebirths until it achieves liberation from the cycle of samsara. Reuniting with loved ones is possible, but not permanent, as the soul may be reborn in different forms and realms[1].

In **Buddhism,** the afterlife is also influenced by one's karma and actions in life. The soul transmigrates through six realms of existence until it attains Nirvana, the state of enlightenment and freedom from suffering. Reuniting with loved ones is also possible, but not permanent, as the soul may move on to different realms and stages of enlightenment[2]

In Native American cultures, the afterlife is often seen as a continuation of life on earth, but in a different dimension or world. The soul remains connected to the natural and spiritual forces and to the ancestors (Reuniting with loved ones is common, as the soul joins the community of the departed and maintains a relationship with the living[3].)

In Mexican culture, the afterlife is a place where the souls of the dead can rest and enjoy the pleasures of life. The souls can also visit the living during **Day of the Dead**, a celebration that honors and remembers the deceased. Reuniting with loved ones is joyful, as the living and the dead share food, music, stories, and offerings[4].

Q. What are the arguments for and against the existence of an immortal soul and a transcendent realm beyond the physical world? Do we really want to know? Why can't we just envisage moving on to Heaven's Hill without thinking too much about science and philosophy?

A. This is a very complex and fascinating topic that has been debated for centuries by philosophers, scientists, theologians, and others. Although there has never been a definitive answer, there have been assumptions that the soul is a distinct and non-physical entity that animates the body and is the source of consciousness, reason, and free will. The soul can exist independently of the body and survive its death[5].

The transcendent realm is a higher and more perfect reality that contains the ideal forms or essences of things, such as beauty, justice, goodness, and so on. The transcendent realm is the true home of the soul and the ultimate goal of its journey[6].

The soul has a natural affinity or attraction to the transcendent realm and can access it through intuition, reason, or mystical experience. The soul can also remember its previous existence in the transcendent realm or its previous incarnations in the empirical world[7]. The soul has a moral obligation or responsibility to seek the transcendent realm and to purify itself from the attachments and illusions of the empirical world. The soul's fate or destiny after death depends on its moral conduct and spiritual progress in life[8,9,10,11]

Some of the arguments against the existence of an immortal soul and a transcendent realm are based on the following premises or assumptions:

- The soul is not a distinct and non-physical entity, but a product or function of the brain and the body. The soul cannot exist independently of the body and ceases to exist when the body dies[12].

- The transcendent realm is not a higher and more perfect reality, but a human construct or projection that reflects our psychological needs and cultural values. The transcendent realm is not the true home of the soul, but a fantasy or illusion that distracts us from the reality of the empirical world[12].

- The empirical world is not a lower and imperfect reality, but the only reality that we can know and experience. The empirical world is not a shadow or reflection of the transcendent realm, but a complex and diverse phenomenon that can offer us many opportunities for learning and enjoyment[12].

- The soul does not have a natural affinity or attraction to the transcendent realm, nor can it access it through intuition, reason, or mystical experience. The soul does not have any memory of its previous existence in the transcendent realm or its previous incarnations in the empirical world, but only of its current life and personal history[12].

- The soul does not have a moral obligation or responsibility to seek the transcendent realm or to purify itself from the attachments and illusions of the empirical world. The soul's fate or destiny after death is irrelevant or unknown, and the only thing that matters is how we live our lives in the present[13].

These are just some of the arguments and evidence that can be considered for and against the existence of an immortal soul and a transcendent realm beyond the physical world. It is my belief, however, that the soul lives on after death, and will take us to our own individual Heaven's Hill.

SEVEN

Joy, Peace and Hope

Death is inevitable, but it is also a mystery. We do not know for sure what happens after we die, or if there is a place where we can reunite with our loved ones who have gone before us. Some people believe in heaven, a realm of peace and joy, and where the righteous are rewarded. Others are skeptical or have different views on the afterlife.

But what if heaven is real, and what if we could meet people there who we loved deeply but who have passed away? How would that feel, and what would that mean for us? This vision is Heaven's Hill.

Think of the joy! Joy is a deep and lasting happiness that comes from within, not from external circumstances. Joy is a fruit of the spirit, a gift that fills our hearts with gratitude and praise. Joy is also a response to love, a love that is unconditional, faithful, and eternal. If we could meet someone on Heaven's Hill who we loved deeply but who has passed away, we could feel joy because we would see them again, face to face, and embrace them with no fear of separation. We could feel joy because we would know that they are safe, happy, and free from pain and sorrow.

Another feeling that we would experience on Heaven's Hill is peace. Peace is a state of calm and tranquility. Peace is a feeling that overcomes fear, doubt, and anxiety. Peace is also a sign of harmony, a harmony that comes from forgiveness, reconciliation, and unity. If we could meet someone in heaven who we loved deeply but who has passed away, we could feel peace because we would have no regrets, no guilt, and no bitterness. We could feel peace because we would have no worries, no troubles, and no conflicts. We could feel peace because we would have no enemies, no rivals, and no threats.

Hope also comes to mind when thinking about Heaven's Hill. Hope is a confident expectation of good things to come. Hope is motivation for living, a living that is purposeful, meaningful, and fruitful. Hope is also a vision for the future, a future that is glorious, wonderful, and eternal. If we could meet someone in heaven who we loved deeply but who has passed away, we would feel hope for the others following us onto Heaven's Hill. We would be reassured that there is life after death and that life is in front of us on Heaven's Hill.

EIGHT

Retaining our Memories

Memory is the ability to store and recall information from past experiences. Memory is essential for learning, problem-solving, and personal identity. However, memory is not a perfect representation of reality, but rather a reconstruction that is influenced by various factors, such as attention, emotion, motivation, context, and interference.

One of the most intriguing aspects of memory is that it can change over time, becoming more or less clear, accurate, or vivid. Sometimes, we can remember incidents and faces from years ago with remarkable clarity, as if they happened yesterday. Other times, we struggle to recall the details of recent events or people we met. Why does this happen, and how does it affect our emotions?

One possible explanation for why some memories are clearer than others is the level of emotional arousal associated with them. Emotions can enhance memory formation and consolidation, especially for events that are personally relevant, surprising, or emotionally intense. This is because emotions trigger the release of hormones and neurotransmitters that activate the brain region involved in emotional processing and memory modulation.

For example, most people can remember where they were and what they were doing when they heard about a major historical event, such as the 9/11 attacks or the COVID-19 pandemic. These events are highly emotional and salient, and they create strong and lasting memories. Similarly, people can often recall the details of their first kiss, their wedding day, or the birth of their child, because these are emotionally significant and meaningful experiences.

However, emotions can also impair memory in some cases, especially when they are too intense or negative. Extreme stress or trauma can interfere with memory encoding and consolidation, leading to memory loss or distortion. This is because excessive stress can impair the functioning of two brain regions involved in memory and executive functions.

For example, people who suffer from post-traumatic stress disorder (PTSD) may experience flashbacks of traumatic events but also have difficulty remembering other aspects of their lives. They may also try to avoid or suppress their traumatic memories, which can further impair their memory and emotional regulation. Similarly, people who experience depression or anxiety may have impaired memory for positive events, but enhanced memory for negative events, creating a biased and distorted view of reality.

Another possible explanation for why some memories are clearer than others is the frequency and quality of retrieval. Retrieval is the process of accessing and reconstructing memories from long-term storage. Retrieval can improve memory by strengthening the connections between the neurons that store the memory traces, making them more resistant to decay or interference. Retrieval can also update and modify memories by incorporating new information or perspectives, making them more adaptive and relevant.

People who frequently rehearse or review their memories, such as by writing a diary, talking to others, or taking photos, can enhance their memory clarity and accuracy. They can also enrich their memories by adding more details, emotions, or meanings to them. Conversely, people who rarely or never retrieve their memories, such as by forgetting, ignoring, or avoiding them, can impair their memory clarity and accuracy. They can also lose some of the details, emotions, or meanings associated with their memories.

The clarity and accuracy of memory can have significant effects on our emotions and well-being. On the one hand, having clear and accurate memories can help us maintain a positive and coherent sense of self, learn from our past experiences, and plan for our future goals. On the other hand, having unclear or inaccurate memories can cause us confusion, frustration, regret, or sadness. Sometimes, we may wish we could remember more of the good times and less of the bad times, or vice versa. Sometimes, we may wonder how reliable our memories are, and how much they reflect the truth or our imagination.

On Heaven's Hill, we retain all our memories and learn to forgive those who have erred against us. We lose feelings of hurt, disappointment, resentment, hatred, and other negative emotions, feeling only happiness and delight at being surrounded by those we have loved and lost over the years. We also begin to feel excited at the expectation of seeing the ones we left behind who will arrive when it is their time to enter Heaven's Hill.

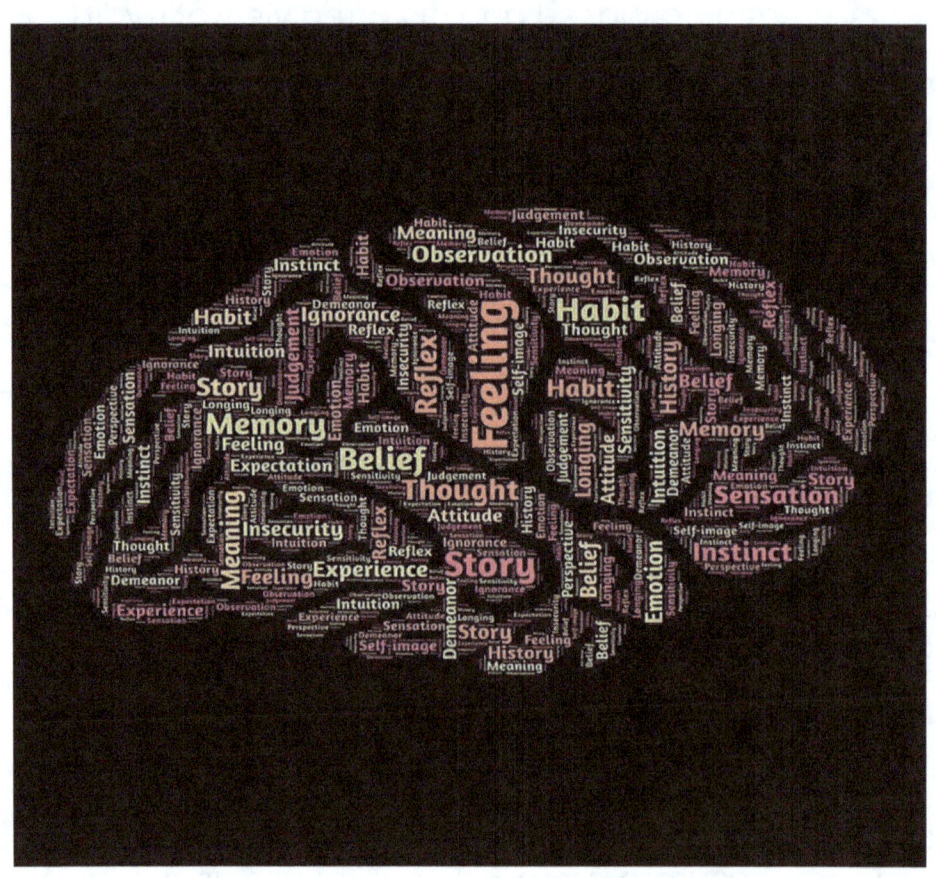

NINE

Souls

The Soul

The concept of the soul has intrigued humanity for centuries, sparking philosophical, religious, and scientific debates. Let's delve into this profound topic, exploring both human and animal souls.

Traditionally, the soul has been associated with a future life and the belief in continued existence after death. It's considered the ultimate animating principle, independent of the physical body. While science has made significant strides in understanding brain function, the reason behind our subjective experiences remains mysterious.

Perspectives

1. **Scientific View:** Some scientists dismiss the soul as just human belief or reduce it to a psychological concept. According to this view, life and death are governed by the laws of chemistry and physics. We're told that we're essentially carbon and proteins, living briefly before returning to stardust.[17]

2. **Biocentrism:** A new theory challenges this model. This new theory challenges the traditional view. It suggests that reality is more complex and that consciousness is essential in shaping it. While it doesn't prove the existence of the soul, it encourages further exploration.

3. **Subjective Experience:** Mysteries like birth, death, dreams, imagination, and memory hint at a vital life force beyond mere physical processes. Perhaps there's a vibrant energy beyond what neuroscience can fully explain.

TEN

Your Own Heaven's Hill

Heaven's Hill is a very personal place that offers each of us an opportunity to see our loved ones, relatives, and old friends, including our greatly missed pets. It's a place that begins in our minds, as we move closer to the end of our lives but opens a realm of possibilities that we might never have explored. Heaven's Hill offers endless, happy scenarios with a feeling of exultation and adventure! Living in the world with expectations of seeing our 'persons' and pets again, can help alleviate the fear of not knowing what follows after we pass on to the next level of life.

Just imagine following a bright light we sometimes hear about, to see an outstretched hand leading you to the open, wonderland of green, rolling hills and soft grass with everyone you have ever known just waiting to greet you. Your fur babies are at the front, of course!

Remember, your Heaven's Hill may be different from mine – it may be a wide expanse of beach and clear, green ocean, or a peaceful setting in the woods sitting on crystal clear lake. No matter what your vision is of Heaven's Hill, it is yours when you are ready to step into it. You no longer have to be afraid – embrace it, and you will be eternally happy. Everyone is waiting for you with open arms!

References

1. (Death and Dying: How different cultures deal with grief and mourning, by John Frederick Wilson, The Conversation). https://phys.org/news/2023-01-death-dying-cultures-grief.html

2. (Legends of the Afterlife: The Various Cultures and Traditions Surrounding Death. Story by Kanita Bajrami). https://www.msn.com/en-us/lifestyle/mind-and-soul/legends-of-the-afterlife-the-various-cultures-and-traditions-surrounding-death/ar-AA1k2DEs.

3. (7 Cultures That Celebrate Death; HISTORY & TRENDS, Words by: Adelle Archer. https://www.eterneva.com/resources/cultures-that-celebrate-death).

4. (The Concept of Afterlife: Understanding the Belief in the Afterlife, by Aamir Khan). https://allaboutgrave.com/the-concept-of-afterlife-understanding-the-belief-in-the-afterlife.

5. (Death Lecture 7 - Plato, Part II: Arguments for the Immortality of the Soul). https://oyc.yale.edu/philosophy/phil-176/lecture-7.

6. (Death Lecture 7 - Plato, Part II: Arguments for the Immortality of the Soul). https://oyc.yale.edu/philosophy/phil-176/lecture-7.). https://www.global-philosophy.org/immortality

7. "Death Lecture 7 - Plato, Part II: Arguments for the Immortality of the Soul." Yale University, https://oyc.yale.edu/philosophy/phil-176/lecture-7. Accessed on 10 July 2024.

8. "PHIL 176: Death Lecture 7 - Plato, Part II: Arguments for the Immortality

of the Soul." Yale University, https://oyc.yale.edu/philosophy/phil-176/lecture-7. Accessed on [current date].

9. Lanza, Robert M.D. "Biocentrism." Robert Lanza Biocentrism, https://www.robertlanzabiocentrism.com/. Accessed on 10 July 2024

10. Lanza, Robert M.D. "Does the Soul Exist? Evidence Says 'Yes'. New scientific theory recognizes life's spiritual dimension." Psychology Today, https://www.psychologytoday.com/us/blog/biocentrism/201112/does-the-soul-exist-evidence-says-yes. Posted December 21, 2011. Accessed on 10 July 2024

11. Global perspectives on death and immortality." Cambridge University Press, https://www.cambridge.org/core/services/aop-cambridge-core/content/view/F04BCC6306A41B78A61A19A5208D94B4/S0034412523000793a.pdf/global-perspectives-on-death-and-immortality.pdf. Accessed on 10 July 2024.

12. "Immortality." Internet Encyclopedia of Philosophy, https://iep.utm.edu/immortal/. Accessed on 10 July 2024.

13. Lanza, Robert M.D. "Does the Soul Exist? Evidence Says 'Yes'. New scientific theory recognizes life's spiritual dimension." Psychology Today, https://www.psychologytoday.com/us/blog/biocentrism/201112/does-the-soul-exist-evidence-says-yes. Posted December 21, 2011. Accessed on 10 July 2024.

14. Hopler, Whitney. "Do Animals Go to Heaven? Afterlife Animal Miracles; Animals Have Souls? Is There an Afterlife Rainbow Bridge for Pets?" Learn Religions, https://www.learnreligions.com/afterlife-animal-miracles-and-heaven-124097. Updated June 25, 2019. Accessed on 10 July 2024.

15. Persephone, Sophia. "Do Animals Have Souls? The Extraordinary Truth." The New Science, https://www.thespiritualscientist.com/2011/02/do-animals-have-souls/. Posted November 2, 2023. Accessed on 10 July 2024.

16. "Do Animals have Souls?" The Spiritual Scientist, https://www.thespiritualscientist.com/2011/02/do-animals-have-souls/. Posted February 24, 2011. Accessed on 10 July 2024.

17. "Science at last explains our Soul." "Explaining the human condition with signs from Science." Damon Isherwood June 27, 2016, Science.

18. Lanza R., Berman B.; Biocentrism: How Life and Consciousness are the Keys to Understanding the True Nature of the Universe, 2009.

HEAVEN'S HILL
MEETING YOUR LOVED ONES
ON THE OTHER SIDE

What happens when we take our final breath?
Where do we go?
Will our loved ones be there waiting?

For centuries, humanity has pondered the mysteries of the Afterlife, searching for reassurance and deeper meaning.

Heaven's Hill: Meeting Your Loved Ones on the Other Side offers a visionary and uplifting guide, helping readers embark on a profound journey toward reuniting with loved ones—including adored pets—who have passed over through the years.

This is not a religious text—it is a compassionate roadmap, blending timeless wisdom with modern insights to ease fears, cultivate mindfulness, and strengthen spiritual bonds.

Whether kept close for comfort or shared with others seeking solace, *Heaven's Hill* invites you to embrace what lies ahead with peace and certainty.
Love transcends time, and those we hold dear are never truly gone—they are simply waiting on the other side.

www.ingramcontent.com/pod-product-compliance
Lightning Source LLC
Chambersburg PA
CBHW081725120626

46550CB00010B/3263